CM0092455O

THE
LAKE DISTRICT

JOHN CURTIS

Text by Richard Ashby

SALMON

INTRODUCTION

It was the growing 18th century awareness of the beauties of nature and the difficulties for travellers on the 'Grand Tour' caused by the wars on the continent which led the leisured classes in England to turn to their own country in search of the 'picturesque'. The first guide book to the Lake District was published in 1778 and over the next two centuries it has been followed by many others, including that by William Wordsworth which ran into many editions. Many writers and artists followed the early travellers and the area is linked to and inspired many who have a distinguished place in cultural England.

The popularity of the Lakes put in danger the very thing that the visitors came to enjoy: the unspoiled beauty, the lonely drama and the peaceful isolation of the mountains and the valleys. Firstly the railways and then the motor car have made the district accessible to many millions.

This conflict was recognised early on. Wordsworth himself proposed in his guide that a National Park should be established to protect and preserve the natural beauties. The National Trust had its birth here, embodied in the late 19th century efforts to prevent the building of a railway through Borrowdale and the conversion of the lakes into reservoirs supplying water to industrial Manchester. The Trust now owns about a quarter of the Lake District and together with the National Park (formed in 1951) has worked hard to preserve and conserve its natural beauties so that it is still possible to experience that sense of awe and wonder which so thrilled the 18th century visitor.

GRANGE-IN-BORROWDALE

The word 'grange' indicates a monastic granary or store. When much of the Lake District was in the hands of the church, the abbey of Furness had two main stores; the other was at Grange-over-Sands. The village is famous for its double-arched stone bridge over the River Derwent and the enormous 'Bowder Stone' not far away.

LODORE FALLS

This spectacular waterfall has been a firm favourite of visitors since the early days of tourism in the Lakes, and ever since those days, too, visitors have been complaining about how tourism is spoiling the place. At one time the local hotel kept a cannon by the lakeside which, for four shillings, would be fired so that visitors could hear the echo rolling around the hillsides.

That attraction is no longer available and at least some peace has returned to this valley.

RYDAL MOUNT, RYDAL

It is perhaps difficult for us today to understand just how popular and successful a poet Wordsworth was in his day. His publications brought financial success too and moving to this impressive house, above Rydal Water, from the small cottage at Grasmere was a significant step up the social ladder.

DORA'S FIELD, RYDAL

Wordsworth purchased this field near Rydal Mount in order to build himself a house. He changed his plans and instead gave it to his daughter Dora. In spring it is a mass of wild flowers, first daffodils and then bluebells, which Wordsworth and his wife planted in Dora's memory.

STICKLE GHYLL, GREAT LANGDALE
The Lake District is a place of contrasts; lush valleys and barren hills are in close proximity. No wonder the early travellers found it so exciting. Stickle Ghyll pours out of Stickle Tarn, with its massive walls of rock, and flows over Dungeon Ghyll Force and down into the quiet loveliness of Great Langdale.

BUTTERMERE
The name 'Buttermere' is given not only to the little village but also to one of the two lakes in the valley. The imposter who bigamously married the 'Maid of Buttermere', a noted beauty, caused something of a 19th century scandal and was eventually hanged for forgery at Carlisle.

AIRA FORCE

'Force' is a common name across the north of England for a waterfall, being derived from the Norse language. Aira Force, above Ullswater, is one of the most beautiful with a drop of over 80ft and spanned by a high arch. There are a number of legends associated with the falls. A Wordsworth poem tells the story of a sleep-walking maiden who, wakened by her knight returning from the wars, falls into the raging torrent.

ULLSWATER

While walking beside the lake with his sister in the spring of 1820, William Wordsworth saw the host of golden daffodils which inspired his most famous poem beginning 'I wandered lonely as a cloud…'

DOVE COTTAGE, GRASMERE

This little house did not have a name when Wordsworth returned to the Lakes from France and came to live here with his sister. It was once an inn known as 'The Dove and Olive Bough'. The name 'Dove Cottage' only dates from 1890, when the house came into the hands of the Wordsworth Trust.

HELVELLYN

Helvellyn is one of the few mountains in England over 3000ft. Although not the highest in the Lakes it is probably the most popular. It is relatively easy to climb and the wonderful views from the summit make it a favourite for hill walkers. Wordsworth took the writer Sir Walter Scott up this majestic peak in 1805.

CASTLERIGG STONE CIRCLE, KESWICK

This prehistoric monument, set on a plateau near Keswick, is believed to date from around 3000 BC and so predates Stonehenge. 18th century visitors, particularly, found it very impressive, and in particular lights and at certain times of the year, it has a powerful and evocative atmosphere.

SURPRISE VIEW, DERWENTWATER

As they drove from Watendlath, in its hidden valley, to Ashness Bridge the early travellers would make a stop and be led to the edge of the hill where this view is suddenly revealed. On a clear day the whole expanse of the lake can be seen, even as far as Keswick, Skiddaw and beyond in the north.

KESWICK AND DERWENTWATER

Keswick was the first of the major Lake District tourist centres. By the late 18th century the beauties of the area had been recognised by a whole host of literary figures and Charles Lamb thought that he had reached fairyland when he saw it.

LITTLE LANGDALE FROM WRYNOSE

The road through Little Langdale and across the Wrynose and Hardknott passes, with its hairpin bends and steep gradients, was only surfaced in 1934. It is hazardous and not to be undertaken in bad weather, but if the weather is fine there are lovely views of the valley.

LOUGHRIGG TARN

This little lake is hidden in a fold of the hills near Grasmere. It was a favourite of William Wordsworth who, associating it with the Roman Goddess, called it 'Diana's Looking-glass'. When the air is still, the sky, surrounding hills, trees and the white-walled cottages are reflected in its tranquil surface.

KIRKSTONE PASS

The main road between Ambleside and Penrith rises to nearly 1500ft above sea level. The road up from Ambleside is so steep it is known as 'The Struggle'. It drops down to the village of Patterdale past Brothers Water, named after two brothers who drowned there one winter after falling through the ice.

LOWESWATER

In the 18th century, with the growing appreciation of the picturesque, it became increasingly fashionable for the wealthy to make the 'Grand Tour' in continental Europe which would usually include the Swiss Alps as well as cities like Rome and Florence. Some guidebooks to the English Lakes suggested that perhaps the shock of first seeing those enormous mountains would be much too great for more delicate English constitutions and that it was necessary to prepare oneself by a visit to these more manageable domestic sights nearer home. Loweswater lies in the peaceful Vale of Lorton. It is off the beaten track and unspoiled in its beauty. There are red squirrels in the area.

BRANTWOOD

The importance of the Victorian artist, writer and critic John Ruskin in the development of English taste cannot be underestimated. He bought Brantwood for its view across Coniston Water to the hill known as 'The Old Man of Coniston'. Ruskin was well-travelled but he believed this view to be the finest in Europe.

TARN HOWS

The smaller lakes in the Lake District are called 'Tarns'. Most are natural, but this one was made in the early 19th century by damming a stream and joining three pools together. It is a very popular place for summer visitors but is best visited in the spring or autumn, when the colours of the surrounding woods are at their most glorious.

CRUMMOCK WATER

This lake shares the valley with Buttermere and is separated from it by the village. It is in an almost secret valley and has a pastoral beauty of its own in spite of the road running through it. Scale Force, which plunges into Crummock Water, is the highest waterfall in the Lake District and was a favourite destination of Victorian visitors.

NEWLANDS VALLEY

Wordsworth knew this valley, and wrote about it in his poem *To May*. He called it 'delicate'. It's lovely pastoral gentleness contrasts strongly with the strength of the surrounding hills. It has not always been so peaceful, for once it was the centre of a quite extensive mining industry. Copper and graphite were worked by German miners but, apart from the pencil industry and its museum at nearby Keswick and some overgrown spoil heaps, nearly everything has disappeared.

BRIDGE HOUSE, AMBLESIDE

The National Trust centre is housed in this former summerhouse built on a bridge which once linked Ambleside Hall to its garden. It is said that at one time it was home to a chair-repairer and his six children; even by the standards of previous centuries it must have been very cramped indeed.

GRIZEDALE FOREST

Between Windermere and Coniston Water the hills are thickly forested. The area was a centre of charcoal burning and later the wood was used for pit props in the Cumberland coal mines. The Forestry Commission now looks after the area and has created a visitor centre with a theatre and cycle and walking trails where artists have made striking sculptures out of wood and other local materials.

S Y GONDOLA, CONISTON WATER

In the *Swallows and Amazons* stories the lake on which the children sail and have their adventures is a combination of Windermere and Coniston Water. The author, Arthur Ransome, knew the area well and lived in a house overlooking Coniston Water. The 'Gondola' is a Victorian steam yacht which has plied the lake since 1860. It sank in a storm in 1963 but has since been restored by the National Trust.

SLATER'S BRIDGE, LITTLE LANGDALE

In such a remote area, with poor roads, communications between the valleys and the outside world were difficult; trade could only be carried on with the use of pack horses or mules. Some of the old tracks have been transformed into modern motor roads but others remain and are used by walkers and ramblers. There are a number of fine pack horse bridges of which Ashness Bridge above Derwentwater, is the best known. Slater's Bridge is unusual in having two spans, one a stone arch, the other a stone slab. It gets its name from the abandoned slate quarries on the hillside above, known as the 'Cathedral'.

HILL TOP, NEAR SAWREY

From her early visits to the Lakes, Beatrix Potter brought back to London pet animals like rabbits and hedgehogs. Peter Rabbit and Mrs Tiggy Winkle come to life in her books. With the profits she bought the farm at Near Sawrey and many of its features and furnishings appear in her pictures.

WASTWATER

The wildness of Wastwater and its
surrounding hills is in complete contrast to the
domesticities of the gentler lakes to the east.
The head of the lake is dominated by the
highest peaks in the Lake District: Yewbarrow,
Great Gable, Lingmell and Sca Fell.

TROUTBECK PARK FARM

The farm nestles at the foot of a rounded hill
called 'The Tongue' which seems to block up
the end of the valley. It is one of the farms
bought by Beatrix Potter with the income
from her famous books and is where she
reared her famous Herdwick sheep.

HAWKSHEAD

This large village, formerly prosperous with the wool and cloth trade and now much frequented by tourists, was Wordsworth's home and where he went to the grammar school after his mother died. Here began the love of the hills and valleys that would be the inspiration for his poetry.

Published in Great Britain by J. Salmon Ltd., Sevenoaks, Kent TN13 1BB. Telephone 01732 452381. Email enquiries@jsalmon.co.uk
Design by John Curtis. Text and photographs © John Curtis. All rights reserved. No part of this book may be produced, stored in a
retrieval system or transmitted in any form or by any means without prior written permission of the publishers.
ISBN 1-902842-59-6   Printed in Italy © 2005

Title page photograph: Bowness-on-Windermere Page two photograph: Skiddaw from Uldale
Front cover photograph: Ashness Bridge Back cover photograph: Rydal Water